Joshua MacNeill

101 Brain Breaks & Brain Based Educational Activities

Calm ▸ Focus ▸ Energize STUDENTS K-12

Table of Contents

Editors: Carolyn Kitchen and Cindy Terry
Photography and Illustration:
iStockphoto and Kate Toussaint
Graphic Design: Ken Van Horn

NeuroLogic®
ACTIVITIES

Acknowledgements

This resource is the result of activities created by Lakeside Youth Service, as well as activities developed from conferences, workshops and books. We owe special thanks to several authors and organizations for giving us permission to use and adapt activities they developed. David Sladkey, who gave us permission to use brain breaks from his book called *Energizing Brain Breaks*. Educational Kinesiology Foundation who gave us permission to use brain breaks from *Brain Gym®*. Finally, the team at Mount Saint Vincent, who gave us permission to use activities from *Dances, Doodles, and Ditties*. *101 Brain Breaks and Brain Based Educational Activities* would not be possible without those who went before us, working to get movement into the classroom. We are hopeful that this will be another step in properly preparing all our students' brains for successful academic experiences.

Beyond the activities themselves, this book is focused a great deal on brain science so that you can determine what brain activities each individual student needs at any given time based on the brain region from which they are operating.   Brain science references in this book are from the work of Bruce D. Perry of the Child Trauma Academy. We owe much of our understanding of the brain to him.

Introduction

Over the past several years, Lakeside Youth Service has been working tirelessly to incorporate trauma informed practices within Lakeside's network of schools. It is impossible to make any real strides toward being trauma informed without first gaining an understanding of how the brain works. As we learned more about the brain, we realized how significantly important it is to prepare students' brains for learning, and to teach in a manner that keeps the brain in mind.

Frequently, we have heard teachers state, "I cannot afford the time to stop and do brain breaks in class." Yet once these same teachers became comfortable implementing these breaks in the classroom, they have affirmed, "I cannot afford not to do brain breaks in my class." Brain breaks are quite simple and can easily become part of the classroom culture. We hope that after looking through this resource, you are excited and prepared to implement brain breaks in your classroom, so that you too can see the amazing impact they have on your students.

How To Use This Resource

This book is organized into two sections: Brain Breaks and Brain Based Educational Activities. Within the Brain Breaks section, you will find three subsections: Calming Activities, Focusing Activities and Energizing Activities. Within the Brain Based Educational Activities section you will also find three subsections: Topic Introduction, Lecture and Note Taking and Review. Please note that there is often overlap. Some brain breaks that calm can also help you focus. Some activities could be used for both topic introduction and review. We categorized the activities where we think they fit best, but feel free to think outside the box and adapt the activities for whatever goal you are attempting to accomplish.

Finally, but perhaps most importantly, you will see for which brain level the brain breaks and brain based educational activities are targeted. One of the key struggles some students have with education is that instruction is focused almost solely on reaching a student's cortex. The problem however, is that if you are anxious, stressed, scared, etc., it is very common to operate from lower brain regions. Feelings of fear, anxiety and stress can be caused by a multitude of things. These feelings can be related to school in general or be in part due to a chaotic home life, a recent traumatic life event, or even childhood trauma. Shortly, we will give a brief explanation of each brain region so that you can predict from which brain region your students are operating. Before we do that, however, we want to give you a quick overview of Brain Breaks and Brain Based Educational Activities.

Understanding Brain Breaks

Presumably, you have heard of brain breaks, otherwise you would not be reading this; however, it is important for you to understand how we define brain breaks. They are quite simply a break for your brain. A brain break is completely separate from the educational content you are working through as the teacher. You are giving your students' brains a chance to process, while simultaneously preparing their brains for the next influx of information by calming them, waking them up, or preparing their brains to focus. The beautiful thing about the brain is that it can continue to process one piece of information while you are focusing your attention on something else.

Understanding Brain-Based Educational Activities

One of the worst ways to learn is to sit and listen to a lecture for an extended period of time. While we have found that brain breaks are an incredible aid in making such learning more effective, we have also found that there are far more brain-friendly ways to teach information. In this section, you will find some different ideas for how to teach your content in a way that will work better with how your students' brains operate. These will take some planning on your part, as you need to insert your class content into them, but we believe you will find that your students' understanding of concepts will grow exponentially when utilizing these activities. We do not view these as an alternative to brain breaks, but rather as a nice complement. If over the course of a class period, you can transition every 10-15 minutes from lecture and note taking to brain breaks and brain based educational activities, you will find a balance that works well with how your students' brains operate.

Brain Regions

The brain is extremely complex, but for our simple understanding, we are going to break it into four regions: Brainstem, Midbrain, Limbic System, and Cortex. When working with students, you want to try to discover from what brain region they are working, and then utilize an activity that will stimulate that region. All of this information is derived from The Neurosequential Model under Bruce D. Perry of the Child Trauma Academy. If you are fascinated by this information, we highly recommend looking into Bruce D. Perry and learning more about the Neurosequential Model.

▓ BRAINSTEM • The brainstem is the lowest region of the brain. This controls many of our most basic functions from breathing to body temperature. For this reason, many of the interventions aimed at the brainstem focus on breathing. Some signs that a student may be working from the brainstem are: they are acting out of reflex without thinking, they are extremely distractible, or they are extremely withdrawn from the rest of the group. The important thing to know about the brain is that it operates from the bottom-up. If your students are operating from their brainstem, an intervention focused on their midbrain or limbic system is not going to help them. You need to focus your activities on their brainstem. Additionally, if a student is working from midbrain, limbic, or even cortex, the brainstem activity will still be beneficial to them because all information travels through the brainstem to get to the other brain regions.

■ MIDBRAIN • Our midbrain primarily controls our movement. A student operating from the midbrain is going to have slightly more self-control than the student in the brainstem, but will still likely be acting out, distractable or withdrawn. A key sign for midbrain issues is to focus on your students' small and large motor skills. As a teacher, you can often watch handwriting change and know you need to do something to stimulate your students' midbrains. Another significant indicator of an issue in the midbrain is when your students are constantly fidgeting or moving around the classroom. Instead of punishing your students for their hyperactivity, try to find a positive opportunity for them to move while remaining in the classroom. In our experience, the midbrain is from where we most often see struggling students operating, and you will see that many of the interventions are focused on stimulating the midbrain.

■ LIMBIC SYSTEM • The limbic system controls our emotions and relationships. Some signs that a student may be operating from the limbic system would be that they are struggling with mood control, having difficulty with some interpersonal relationships, or are giving emotional / relational responses to non-emotional events. A classic example is the student who turns being told they can't go to bathroom into a reason for accusing you of hating them. Interventions that help the limbic system are group or partner activities that have students working together or with you to achieve a common goal. Additionally, activities that make students more aware of and in tune with one another will help to stimulate the limbic system.

▦ CORTEX • The cortex is the highest brain region. You will notice that none of the activities are focused on the cortex because in a way, these activities and all of your teaching are focused on the cortex. By activating the lower brain regions, you are helping to gain access to the cortex where higher-level thinking and information storage can occur. Remember the bottom-up functionality of the brain. You must discover ways of stimulating lower regions of the brain first, or else you will struggle to reach the cortex.

Final Thoughts

You will see that many of the activities involve breathing. Breathing is an extremely important component to prepare our brains to learn since our hearts and brains are intricately connected. Checking your pulse can be a great barometer for the condition of your brain, and breathing exercises are a great way to bring the pulse back down. One of the goals of the breathing exercises is to breathe from your belly. When we belly breathe instead of chest breathe, we get ten times as much air into our bodies, allowing for greater oxygen flow to our brains and thus better brain functioning.

In addition to breathing exercises, one of our favorite things to do is include activities where students will cross their midline. Your body has this invisible line dividing your right half from your left half. When you have body movements that cause you to cross your body's midline, you activate both hemispheres of your brain and thicken the connecting fiber of neural pathways called the corpus callosum. We have seen crossing the midline have a great impact on student learning. We noted each activity that included this movement.

One word of caution, many of the activities in this resource could easily have a competitive component to them. We highly recommend that you proceed cautiously when including competition. You know your students best. With some students, adding in competition will be the piece that helps them to buy-in and get involved with activities. With some students, however, the possibility of losing will actually do more harm than good. If you think your students will struggle with it, steer them away from competitive activities and keep it simple. To see some of the activities from this resource acted out, check out: lakesidelink.com/training/brainbreaks.

Brain Breaks

Opportunities to give your students a brief break from the educational content and prepare their brains to learn.

Calming Breaks

Box Breathing

Adapted from *Doodles, Dances and Ditties*

Brainstem

Breathe in through your nose for a count of four, hold your breath for a count of four, then exhale through your mouth for a count of four. Repeat for 2-4 minutes. This helps to regulate breathing and calm you down. It may help to draw a box with your finger on your desk or a large box in the air out in front of your body as you breathe.

Six Second Breathing

Adapted from *Doodles, Dances and Ditties*

Brainstem / Midbrain

Sway your body slowly back and forth and inhale while counting to six. While you are counting slowly, bring your arms up over your head, then exhale counting backwards from six and slowly bring your arms back down. Repeat for 2-4 minutes. This helps to regulate breathing and calm you down.

Nostril Breathing

Brainstem

Put your right index finger over your left nostril; take a long breath in from you right nostril. Now, remove your right finger from your left nostril, and put your left index finger on your right nostril and slowly breathe out. Then take another deep breath in through your left nostril, and repeat the cycle. Essentially, you do a pattern of deep breaths out then in from the same nostril, then switch nostrils, always covering your nostril with the opposite hand. This crossover allows you to cross your midline. (This sounds far more complicated than it is.)

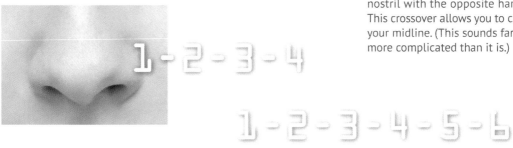

Mindful Breathing

Brainstem

Take one minute of absolute silence and just think about your breathing. How does it feel? Where do you feel it? How does breathing in feel different than breathing out? Can you control where your breath goes once it is inside of you? This exercise helps calm you down.

Belly Breathing

Brainstem

Please read about belly breathing in the "How To Use This Resource" section. Two exercises to help force belly breathing are as follows. Lace your hands behind your head and breathe, or reach your hands as far as you can behind your back and breathe. Doing this opens up your ribcage, forcing air to come down into your belly.

Progressive Breathing

Brainstem

This is a great way of practicing control over your breathing. Take a deep breath in for a count of two then breathe it out for a count of two. Then breathe in for a count of four and then out for four. Work your way up in two second intervals to a count of eight.

IN

OUT

DEEP

INHALE

EXHALE

Object Breathing

Brainstem / Midbrain

For this breathing exercise, have your students move an object around on their desks by breathing on it. You can keep it simple and have them blow a cotton ball around or a small wad of paper. You can add more control by drawing a path or putting cards on their desk for where they need to attempt to blow the object

Paper Football Breathing

Brainstem

Make a paper football. If you have never done this before, you take a long strip of paper and fold it repeatedly into a triangle; at the end you can tuck it into itself. Typically, with a paper football, you flick your triangle and try to get it to hang over the edge on the opposite side of the desk / table. In this version, instead of flicking, use your breath to move the football down the field. You can either have students play against each other or alone at their desk, adding up their touchdowns.

Hum, Hum, Hum

Adapted from *Doodles, Dances and Ditties*

Brainstem

You can use humming a few different ways. You can hum your favorite songs, hum together as a class, or even have humming conversations where you hum words instead of speaking with one another. Humming is bene-ficial as it forces you to take a deep breath and slowly exhale as you hum your breath out. As you hum, it vibrates your face, loosening some of those muscles that tense up when you get angry or stressed.

hummmmmmmmmmmmm...

Bubble Blowing

Adapted from *Doodles, Dances and Ditties*

Brainstem / Midbrain

Any attention to breathing is going to be beneficial, and blowing bubbles is an excellent example of that. Blowing bubbles causes you to control your breathing and take some deep breaths. A simple bubble container can be a great way to help your students reset during the middle of class. You could also add some creative activities with popping the bubbles if you wanted to get a little more involved in the midbrain.

Stretching

Midbrain

Taking a moment to stand up and do a couple of arm and leg stretches is a great way to get blood flowing and relax some of the tension that learning can bring. Try some stretches that cause you to cross your body's midline for an added bonus.

Origami

Midbrain

Take a break and do some sort of origami together as a class. Choose something simple that can be done in just a few minutes. If you do not know any origami, you can easily find instructions online. If you find that your class enjoys this, you could try taking origami breaks where you do little bits at a time of a much more intricate project. You could add a limbic dimension to this by making it a full class project that will ultimately be put together.

17

Hook-Ups

Adapted from *Brain Gym®*

Brainstem / Midbrain

While sitting or standing, cross your legs, extend your arms out with your hands back to back and thumbs down. Put one arm over the other and interlock your fingers. Then bend your elbows, bringing your interlocked fingers down and then up to your chest. Hold this position for a minute or so. This position has you crossing your midline multiple times, helping both hemispheres of your brain to communicate. Additionally, this exercise causes you to essentially swaddle yourself, which helps to stimulate the brainstem. During this exercise, encourage your students to take slow breaths, or even add in a breathing brain break. Additionally, you can have students hold this position while you're teaching, and not limit it to a brain break.

Isometrics

Midbrain

There are many different isometric exercises you can do. A few easy ones to try are listed here. If you find that your students enjoy these exercises, you can look up many more online. Put hands palm to palm (like praying) and press hard against each other. Hold hands like an opera singer, and pull fingers apart for a few seconds. Clasp hands together and stretch them as high as possible. Shrug shoulders up to neck. One at a time, put each hand to its corresponding knee and press against each other. Put one foot on top of the other and push against each other then switch. Repeat each of these exercises 3-5 times in a row for a few seconds each. Don't feel like you need to work through all of them in one day. These help regulate the brain and organize lower brain functions.

Face Massages

Brainstem / Midbrain

Our faces change as our emotions change. The more stressed or anxious we get, the more tense the muscles in our face become. Taking a moment to massage our faces, especially our foreheads and cheekbones, can help to relax those muscles and consequently, relax your demeanor.

Doodling

Midbrain

Many students are already doodling; give them a moment to doodle where you are not trying to teach them. If you want to turn this into a brain based educational activity, you can have your students doodle something that somehow relates to the content you have been teaching in class, or have them doodle their notes instead of writing regular notes.

Paper Airplanes

Midbrain

Give each of your students a blank piece of paper and tell them they have thirty seconds to make their best paper airplane. Then quickly line up all of your students to simultaneously throw their airplanes across the room. You can turn this into a little competition to see whose goes farthest or keep it as simple fun. Between the fine motor skills of folding the plane and the large muscle movement of throwing the plane, you get the full spectrum of beneficial movements for your midbrain.

Lazy 8s

Adapted from *Brain Gym®*

Midbrain

Hold a thumb up about 10-12 inches centered in front of your face. Using this as the center point, draw an infinity sign in front of your face with your thumb. Don't move your head but follow your thumb with your eyes. The movement should be slow and controlled, and the sign should be between 12 and 16 inches wide. Do it multiple times with each hand, then bring your hands together and do it several more times. This movement crosses your midline and prepares your eyes and brain to read.

19

Rhythm: Call and Response

Brainstem / Midbrain / Limbic

You can either lead this yourself or have a student lead it. Have the leader tap a simple rhythm on their desk or lap, and then have the rest of the class repeat it all together. Do this multiple times with different rhythms. You can give different students the chance to lead.

Opposite Thumb Twiddles

Adapted from *Energizing Brain Breaks*

Midbrain

Interlock your fingers and spin your thumbs around one another. Now try a little spin on this. Rotate one thumb forward while rotating the other thumb backwards. This is more difficult and causes you to put a lot of brainpower into the activity.

Hand Crossing Mix-up

Adapted from *Energizing Brain Breaks*

Midbrain

Extend your arms out in front of your body. Now cross your left hand over your right hand. Attempt to spin your left hand in circles going clockwise while spinning your right hand in circles going counterclockwise. If you master this, or get fed up with it, you can try bobbing one hand straight up and down while bobbing the other left and right. A final variation would be to spin one hand while trying to move the other one either up and down or left and right. This activity is great for transitions as it takes a lot of focus on a small task. All of the midline crossing is great for your brain.

Focusing Breaks

Paper Balance

Adapted from *Energizing Brain Breaks*

Midbrain

Give each student a sheet of paper, have them place it on the palm of their hand with their hand flat and palm up. They cannot grip the paper or tilt their hands at all. From here you can have them do a few different activities. They can try to pass the paper from hand to hand behind their back, they can do figure eights with the paper around their legs, or they can try walking around the classroom without letting the paper fall. It seems fairly easy, but the wind resistance of one sheet of paper causes it to fly readily, forcing the students to have to move more slowly and cautiously than they may want to.

Thumb Pinkie Switch

Adapted from *Energizing Brain Breaks*

Midbrain

Put your right hand out in front of your body and give thumbs up. Then put your left hand out next to it, and stick only your pinkie out. Swap back and forth which hand has a pinkie out and which one has the thumb out. See how quickly you can do it.

Nose and Ear Reversal

Adapted from *Energizing Brain Breaks*

Midbrain

Have your students place the pointer finger of their right hand on the tip of their nose and the pointer finger of their left hand on their right earlobe. Then, as quickly as they can, have them move their right pointer finger to their left ear, and their left pointer finger to their nose. When they do the swap, they also need to switch which wrist is overlapping the other. Keep switching back and forth as quickly as you can.

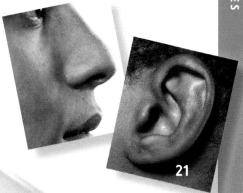

Scissor Winks

Midbrain

Simultaneously wink your right eye and, using your pointer finger and middle finger to make a pair of scissors, scissor snip with your left hand once. Then switch, and wink your left eye while scissor snipping with the fingers on your right hand. Try to repeat this routine ten times in a row.

Finger Gaps

Midbrain

Have your students place one of their hands flat on their desk with fingers spread apart as wide as they can. Using either their pointer finger, or the eraser end of a pencil, have them tap the desk between their finger gaps. Encourage them to go down the line and back as fast as they can without ever poking their fingers. Once they have mastered that hand, have them switch hands and try again.

ABC / 123

Adapted from *Energizing Brain Breaks*

Midbrain

Ask students to count as they draw large letters in the air with their index fingers. As they say "1", they will be drawing an "A". When they say "2", they will be drawing a "B." See if they can get to Z and be at the number 26.

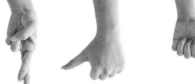

Chime Focus Stand

Midbrain / Limbic

Have your class be completely silent. Then using a chime or a bell (there are even chime apps available on your phone), start a note, and have your students listen intently. The moment they stop hearing the sound they should stand immediately. This is a great activity for increasing focus and making each student aware of one another's focus as a group. Do this several times and watch as the group becomes more unified in their responses. You can ask them to shut their eyes so they do not see others preparing to stand.

Twisted Hands

Adapted from *Energizing Brain Breaks*

Midbrain

Have your students stick their hands straight out in front of their bodies with their fingers out and thumb down. Now have them put one hand over the other so that their palms are touching. Now have them fold their hands, lacing their fingers together. Finally, have them keep their fingers linked and fold their hands in to their chest. (This sounds complicated, but once you figure it out, it is quite simple.) Then call out which finger you want them to wiggle: "right index finger, left middle finger", etc. It is a fun activity that is harder than it looks. You can also have them partner up and have one student point at the finger they want the other one to wiggle. Just make sure they don't touch it, as it makes it easier to wiggle the correct one.

Hand-Motion Chains

Midbrain / Limbic

Choose one student to start; they need to do one random hand motion. They can be as creative as they want coming up with their hand motion. Then go around the room one-by-one, repeating the hand motions done before you, and adding a new one. It should eventually come all the way back to the first person who needs to do their best to do the whole line of hand motions in order. This is a great way to work on focus and short term memory, not to mention that students will inevitably do hand motions that cross the midline and may even challenge the brain in other ways. If you add saying the student's name before the hand motion each student came up with, you can help build a bit more classroom camaraderie.

Opposite Arm Rolls

Adapted from *Energizing Brain Breaks*

Midbrain

Bend your right arm out in front of you and begin turning it in circles that go away from your body. While your right arm is still moving, try to put your left arm in front of your body and turn it in a circle going the opposite direction.

Behind Your Back Catches

Midbrain

You can use almost any object for this: a ball, fidget, pen, paperclip, etc. Simply ask the students to toss the object up in the air and attempt to catch it behind their backs. Some people master it quickly; others never do, but it is usually good for a laugh.

Air Letter Stories

Adapted from *Doodles, Dances and Ditties*

Midbrain / Limbic

Have your students partner up to tell one another either about last weekend or plans for the upcoming weekend (you could really have them tell each other anything). Instead of verbally telling the story, have students write the story in big air letters in front of them. Once they are done, have the student who was not telling the story try to guess what was said. This is a great exercise in paying attention and communicating with others, as well as a great opportunity to get large muscle movement and midline crossing.

–and then...

Ball Toss Focus Clap

Midbrain / Limbic

In front of the classroom, where everyone can see you, pick an object that you are going to throw up in the air. If you do not have a ball, it can be anything you can catch without it breaking. When you throw it up in the air, tell your students to clap once when they think that the object has reached it's highest point and is ready to come down. Toss it up several times and watch how much more unified your class becomes. Try to trick them a little with very short throws and some higher ones. This activity does a great job focusing your students and helps make them aware of one another as they zero in their focus. It really doesn't matter if you have a low ceiling, though there will be less variations in your heights. Try tossing the object from a sitting position to

give it more variance. If the object bounces, you can also have them clap when it hits the floor.

Silent Line Up

Limbic

Tell your students to line up according to your instructions but without verbally communicating to each other. Some ideas for how to order them are: height, birthday, alphabetical order for first, middle, or last name, etc. This helps students to work with one another and makes them a little more aware of the power of their nonverbal communication.

NeuroLogic® ACTIVITIES

Energizing Breaks

Mirroring Motions

Adapted from *Doodles, Dances and Ditties*

Limbic

Have each student partner up and stand facing his or her partner. Choose one person to start as the leader. This person should move all around in a controlled fashion, moving hands, feet, arms, etc. The other person has to try to mirror the actions as well as possible. After a minute, switch and let the other person lead. The key to this is keeping the movement controlled. If you want to make it simpler, only allow hand motions. This is great for helping students focus, learn personal space, and interact positively with one another.

Lion's Breath

Adapted from *Doodles, Dances and Ditties*

Brainstem

Take a deep breath in. Then open your mouth as widely as you can, stick your tongue out and down towards your chin, and release all your breath with a roar like a lion. Repeat several times. This helps wake you up and will likely be good for a laugh.

Random Noise Breathing

Brainstem

For this activity, have each of your students take a deep breath. As they exhale, have them make the most random / funny / goofy noise they can think of. Repeat as needed. Not only is this focus on breathing a beneficial practice, but this is almost guaranteed to cause some laughter (and laughter is excellent for the brain and self-regulation).

Rock Paper Scissors

Midbrain / Limbic

Have your students stand up and play a game of rock paper scissors with as many people in the room as possible. You could time this or create an end goal with a winner. End goals could be: first person to win three rounds, first person to play a round with everyone, etc. This is a great way to get your students up and moving around, as well as a great way to initiate interaction between students.

Pushing Down the Line

Midbrain / Limbic

Have your class line up in two equal lines facing each other. Each person should be directly across from another and close enough that they could comfortably reach out and touch palms. The goal is for your students to pass a book down the line by only pressing the palms of their hands on the book. The book must stay upright and they cannot put their hands underneath it. They just need to moderate how hard they are pressing the book against the other person's hand. This activity is great for the limbic system as it forces you to be very aware of the person across from you, as well as the fact that you are working with everyone in your class to accomplish a single goal. It is also great for large muscle movement and crossing the midline. Once they have mas-

tered it with one book, add some more. My one class successfully sent seven books down the line.

Ball Tossing

Midbrain

A simple break to stop class and toss an object around, such as a small ball, is a great way to activate your midbrain, and to help kick start your students' focus on something simple. Sometimes I use my 2½-minute gel timer and see how many catches my class can get in a row before dropping the ball. When we do this, I occasionally put each class's total up on the board to have them compete with other classes throughout the day.

Switch-Change-Rotate

Limbic

Put students in a straight line, preferably 4-5 in the line. When you say, "switch," the person from the front of the line moves to the back of the line. When you say, "change," the person in the front of the line switches places with the person in the back of the line. And when you say, "rotate," everyone turns around, making the person who was first last and last first. Rapidly call out different commands in no particular order. This helps to wake up students and prepare them to learn, as their brains have to quickly change roles and figure out what they need to do according to the verbal commands.

Gotchya

Adapted from *Energizing Brain Breaks*

Limbic / Midbrain

Have your class stand in a big circle around the room. They should be able to reach the person next to them. Have everyone put their left hand out, palm up, almost like they were a waiter carrying an invisible tray. Now, have everyone take their right hand, and touch their pointer finger to the palm of the hand of the person to their right. When you say go, they need to simultaneously attempt to grab the finger of the person on their left, while trying to not get their finger grabbed by the person on their right. If you successfully grab the person's finger, you shout, "Gotchya." This is great for increasing focus and being aware of everything that is going on around you.

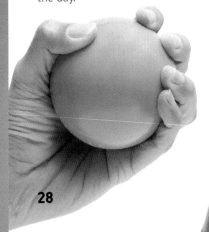

Chair Sit-Ups

Midbrain

Have your students sit upright and place their hands on their seats. Have them push hard on the seat in an attempt to lift up their bodies. A quick ten reps is a great way to get blood flowing and prepare students to move forward with the rest of the class period.

Secret Handshakes

Midbrain / Limbic System

A quick and simple version of this is to have your students quickly partner up and create a secret handshake. Tell them how many moves you want in it. This can be done in 30 seconds. There are a few variations you can try. The day after doing secret handshakes, you can have them partner up again and see if they remember. You can have them create the handshake, then switch partners and teach the secret handshake to someone else. Finally (and my personal favorite) have them create a secret handshake using only their right hand; then have them attempt to duplicate it with only their left hand. It's tricky but causes them to work on their focus.

Balance Beam Tape Trail

Midbrain

Using a tape that your school approves of for placing on the floor, create a trail around the room. It is up to you if you want to make it simple or complicated with obstacles. Take a break to have your students walk the beam around the room trying not to step off the tape. You can have your students make the trail as a brain break sometime, but be warned it will take a little bit of time.

Desk Turns

Midbrain

This is a perfect reminder that brain breaks do not have to be complicated. If your teaching and classroom allows, move to another wall and have your students all stand up and turn their desks to keep facing you. If you are teaching from one location, have them each stand up, pick up their desk or chair, and do a 360 degree turn. The large muscle movement in heavy lifting is great to either calm down the hyper student or wake up the tired or withdrawn student.

Card Throwing Competition

Midbrain

Buy a deck of cards with which you are willing to never actually play. Give each student a card, or a couple cards. Have all your students get on one side of the room and attempt to throw their cards all the way across the room. The movement most people use to throw a card often causes them to cross their midline, which is an added bonus. You need to know your students well before attempting this activity and set it up in a way that will keep everyone safe.

Energy Breathing

Adapted from *Doodles, Dances and Ditties*

Brainstem / Midbrain

Put your hands out in front of your body as you prepare to take some deep breaths. Rub your hands together vigorously as you inhale, then tap your fingertips together repeatedly as you exhale. Repeat for 2-4 minutes. This helps wake you up.

Woo Wah Wish

Midbrain / Limbic

Have students sit in a circle. Using some kind of soft ball, have students throw the ball to each other. If you throw the ball to the person directly to your right, you have to say, "woo." If you throw the ball to the person to your left, you have to say, "wah." And if you throw the ball to anyone else you must say, "wish." You cannot have any two of the same throws in a row, (if the person who threw you the ball said, "wish" you have to do either a "woo" or a "wah.") This helps to wake up the brain by causing the student to think about what they will do if they get the ball next. Additionally, the large muscles used in throwing can help to calm you down and regulate you.

Woo →
← Wah
Wish

Tap Your Tude

Adapted from *Doodles, Dances and Ditties*

Brainstem / Midbrain

Ask your students to tap, either on their lap or their desk, in a manner that represents how their attitude is at the moment. You can do this as a gauge of their attitudes. Afterwards, you can lead them in a calm and soothing rhythm and have all of your students meet you there. It can be a fun way to express yourself and a great way to begin moving your large muscles in a way that can activate your midbrain.

NeuroLogic ACTIVITIES

Imaginary Catch

Adapted from *Doodles, Dances and Ditties*

Midbrain / Limbic

Have your students quickly partner up, and with an imaginary ball of their choice, commence an imaginary catch. In my experience, this quickly turns into some of the best catches in history, and you don't have to worry about a stray ball breaking a computer screen. Even this simple act between two people can be a positive interaction for someone's limbic system.

Air Instruments

Midbrain

Give your students 30 seconds to jam out on the air instrument of their choice. If you are not familiar with the idea of an "air guitar" it just means an imaginary one. They pretend to play an instrument. This can cause some fun large muscle movement and is a great way to get some blood flowing. If you wanted to add a breathing / brainstem component, you could make it strictly woodwind instruments where they are breathing deeply as they pretend to blow into the instruments and play. Just a warning: they may not enjoy stepping away from their air drums to play the air flute. Good luck.

Random Object Towers

Midbrain / Limbic

Put your students in small groups and have them build a tower on their desk with whatever materials they can find around the room that are not breakable. If you would struggle to trust your students' selections, you can supply them with some teacher approved random objects and let them build.

Stand Up–Turn Around–Sit Down

Midbrain

Don't put too much thought into this. Stand up, turn around, and sit down. Just a quick burst of oxygen to the brain is sometimes all your students nee You could also have them wal quick lap around the room a en sit back down. Someti he best ideas are the simpl

Dance Party

Midbrain

Crank up your favorite school appropriate song, and let your students participate in a three-minute dance party. This is a great way to get some energy out, let some oxygen flow to your brain, and have a little creative outlet.

Human Airplane

Midbrain

Simply extend your arms out like wings and fly around the room like an airplane. This is obviously just a more creative way of walking around the room to get blood flowing through your veins and oxygen to your brain. Bringing out the imaginative little child in each of your students can be very calming as you move into teaching them difficult academic material.

NeuroLogic® ACTIVITIES

33

Conduct The Song

Midbrain

Play any school appropriate song and have your students act as the conductor and conduct the music. The best part of this is that they do not need any actual musical talent. It is a great way to get up and move your large muscles around. Additionally, your students will likely be crossing their midlines as they conduct the music. You can have your whole class do this at once or let one student come to the front of the room and lead. If you have one student lead, you could merge this activity with the air instruments and let the rest of the class play along.

Thumb Ball for Brain Breaks

Midbrain

If you have never seen one before, thumb-balls are essentially stuffed mini soccer balls. You can purchase blank ones or get them with questions written on them. I recommend purchasing blank ones or a similar style ball that is blank, and fill in each hexagon with a number. Then, for each number, write a corresponding question. You can keep these questions as light and easy to respond to as you want: favorite vacation, favorite car, favorite food, etc. You could also try either/or questions: Pepsi or Coke, city or country, summer or winter, etc. Once you have your ball set up, take a five-minute break to toss the ball around the class. Whatever question your right thumb is on when you catch the ball is the question you need to answer.

Make It Snow

Adapted from *Energizing Brain Breaks*

Brainstem / Midbrain

Give each student a sheet of paper. Let them rip it up into as many pieces as they can in one minute. Then on the count of three, let every student blow their pile of paper off the desk. Once they have finished enjoying the opportunity to make it snow in class, give them another minute to clean up the mess.

Brain Based Educational Activities

Teaching with the brain in mind.

NeuroLogic® ACTIVITIES

Topic Introduction

One Footed Responses

Midbrain

This is a very simple activity that can be used for either introducing a new topic or for review. As a teacher, you prepare questions that are either "yes" or "no", "true" or "false", "agree" or "disagree." Assign one answer to the left foot and one to the right. Have all your students stand and respond by balancing on the corresponding foot. This is fairly non-threatening as most students will not be able to quickly see everyone else's responses, but as a teacher, you can get a quick idea of where everyone is. Having the students stand is great for getting the blood pumping, and balance is a good way to work the midbrain and increase the connection of both halves of the brain.

Jumping Responses

Midbrain

This is a very simple activity that can be used for introducing a new topic or for review. As a teacher, you prepare questions that are either "yes" or "no", "true" or "false", "agree" or "disagree." Have all your students stand up: if they agree, or would answer yes or true to your statement, they are to jump, if they disagree or would answer no or false, they should sit down. Having the students sit, stand, and jump is great for getting the blood pumping, and you will see very quickly where everyone is at with the material you are covering.

Answers Around The Room

Midbrain

Post short answer questions on sheets of paper around the room. These can be introductory opinion questions or review questions. Have the students walk around the room and respond to at least three of the questions. Moving around the room is great for blood flow. Additionally, writing on large sheets of paper usually involves crossing your midline.

Breathing Answers

Brainstem

Dedicate different areas of the student desk to different responses. You can do this by writing on the desk or by taping index cards to the desk. Then give each student a cotton ball or small wadded up piece of paper. With each question, have the student move the ball to the correct answer using only their breath.

Agree / Disagree Conversations

Midbrain / Limbic

Designate the four corners of the room as different levels of agreement. Strongly agree, agree, disagree, and strongly disagree. Make some statements that relate to the new topics you will be covering in class, and have each student walk over to the corner that best represents their response to the statement. Once each student has chosen the corner that best represents their position, have a group conversation where your students share why they went to the corner they chose.

First Impressions

Midbrain

When beginning a new unit or new topic, pick a handful of key words that you will be teaching. This activity is a form of word association, where instead of them saying the first thing that comes to mind, they are to act out the first thing that comes to mind when you say the new term. If you want to start simple, you could start with facial expressions and work your way up to full on acting.

Order of Operation
- **P**lease
- **E**xcuse
- **M**y
- **D**ear
- **A**unt
- **S**ally

NeuroLogic ACTIVITIES

Lecture and Note Taking

Notes Around The Room

Midbrain

Instead of having all your Power-Point slides on the projector, print them out and post them around the room. Have your students then travel around the room to take notes. You could either travel with them to do the lecture aspect as they walk around the room, or lecture them once they have it all written out to fill in any blanks. This is a great way to keep the students moving around as they learn. Another way to do this is to give the students worksheets where the answers can be found in the notes posted around the room. You could still do this as initial notes or as a review activity.

Snowball Questions

Adapted from *Energizing Brain Breaks*

Midbrain

You can either supply your class with sheets of paper for questions, or let them rip out a sheet of paper from their notebooks. When they have a question, instead of raising their hand, they write it down, ball it up, and throw it up to the front of the room. Throwing is a large muscle movement that can get a great pump of oxygen to the brain, but can also be a safe way to ask a question. As a teacher, it gives you a little control to glance at the question and either stop class then and answer it, or say, "great question, we are actually getting to this in a couple minutes." It may seem weird at first and you will feel like a target, but you will quickly find that it becomes normal.

Group Summaries

Limbic

Break your students up into smaller groups. Assign each member of the group a section of the reading to read individually. This could be different parts of a chapter, an article, or a section in a textbook, etc. Then, have them work together as a group to share their sections with one another and write a summary for the entire reading.

Popcorn Reading And Throwing

Midbrain / Limbic

If you would typically do popcorn reading in your class, add a twist to it by tossing a ball or fidget to whomever the student is calling on to read next. Still have the students name the person, but they are additionally throwing something. This helps to use a little bit of large muscle movement and focus in order to catch the ball.

Paper Airplane Questions

Midbrain

You can either supply your class with sheets of paper for questions, or let them rip out a sheet of paper from their notebooks. When they have a question, instead of raising their hand, they write it down, fold the paper into a paper airplane and throw it up to the front of the room. The fine motor skills used in folding is great for the midbrain, and sometimes in the time it would take to fold the airplane, you end up answering the question, or they realize they no longer need to ask it. This little throw is a great pump of oxygen to the brain but can also be a safe way to ask a question. As a teacher, it gives you a little control to glance at the question and either stop class then and answer it, or say, "great question, we are actually getting to this in a couple minutes." It gives the

teacher a little more control in how they are going to operate the class and navigate the incoming questions. It will seem weird at first and you will feel like a target, but you will quickly find that it becomes normal.

Looping Notes

Midbrain

Provide your students with long slips of paper to write their notes on. For each new idea or new term, have them write on a separate slip of paper. Either as you are going, or once you are all finished, have them glue or tape each slip in a loop and connect the loops like a chain. If you are teaching something that needs to occur in a certain sequence, be sure to have them link the loops in the correct order. You can hang these chains around the room as a visual reminder of what was discussed.

Jingle Notes

Midbrain / Limbic

While teaching, or immediately after teaching a new concept, stop and have the students partner up and write a rap or jingle that explains the point that was just taught. Have each group share with the rest of the class. You can even have the class vote on their favorite.

Desk Answers

Midbrain

Many desks are actually made out of a material on which a dry erase marker may be used. If your desks are not like this, put a poster board on each student's desk. While taking notes, allow them to write really big on their desk, or while doing a review game, allow them to write their answers really big on their desks. These larger movements are great for the midbrain and increase the likelihood that they may cross their midline while working. Additionally, the novelty of writing on their desks will likely help them remember the information later for a test or a quiz. If you do this, you may want to hand out a printed version of notes for the day so students have something to take with them. Be prepared with paper towels to clean off the desks.

Key Point Charades

Midbrain / Limbic

This can be done in one of two ways. The first way is for you as the teacher to do the charades. As you are teaching a concept, use charades to get your students to guess by your movements the description of what you are teaching them. The other version is for a student to do the charades. You give a student a key concept from what you are teaching, and have them act it out charades-style to see if the other students can guess what they are depicting. I know this seems like it would be easier in some subject areas than others, but you may be surprised with some of the creative ideas students come up with for portraying different concepts.

Building Block Notes

Midbrain

Give your students some type of building block. This could be wooden blocks or any other type of stackable material that they can write on. As you teach, have them take notes on the blocks. Have them write foundational information on the bottom blocks, and then build upon it with more information until they have a small tower built. This can be great in math or science to teach the order that some formulas require, or in history or English to teach about cause and effect. If you do this, you may want to hand out a printed version of notes for the day so they have something to take with them. A set of blocks can stay in your classroom as a visual reminder of the concepts learned.

Image Outline Notes

Midbrain

Instead of having your students use standard lined paper to take notes, give them a sheet of paper with an outline of an image that represents something within the lesson you are teaching. Have the students take notes however they want on this paper with the image. They could color it in, write around the outline, write inside the image, etc. Giving them this creative decision can be a great way to stimulate their midbrain and cortex while taking notes.

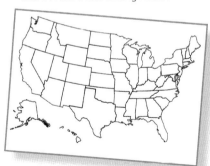

41

Review

Cartoon Notes

Midbrain

While teaching, instead of giving traditional lined paper, give students paper with blank comic strips and ask them to write a comic about what they are learning instead of simple notes. This allows them to get a little more creative with their notes and can show whether or not they really understand the content. You may want to consider leaving this as an option for students who would like to try it, or supplying your own notes at the end of the class for anyone who struggles to decipher what they meant by their cartoon. The use of creative arts is a great way to work with the midbrain.

Standing In Sequence

Midbrain / Limbic

Supply each student with a card that has a piece of information on it. This could be an event from a book, an event in history, an operation in math, or a science problem. Have the students line themselves up in the correct sequence based on the card that they have. If you want to add some difficulty to this, you could give the students limited time or take away the ability to speak.

Beat Review

Brainstem / Midbrain

Teach your students four different short beats; this could be on their laps, desk, clapping, or a combination of each. Have each beat represent one of A, B, C, and D for multiple-choice questions. Then ask multiple-choice questions, and have them respond with the beat of the correct answer.

Fourscore and...

Team Review Toss

Midbrain / Limbic

Break your class into two teams. Ask review questions. Whichever teams answers correctly first gets to attempt to toss a ball into a basket. (You could easily use a clean trashcan or empty box, etc.) If they score, they get a point. The team with the most points at the end wins.

Hidden Answers

Midbrain

Give each student a review question or a couple of review questions. Around the room "hide" answers to each question. Each student needs to search around the room and find their correct answer. This is a great way to get them up and moving. Depending on the content and how closely related all the answers are, this may turn into a limbic activity as the students communicate with one another as to which answers go with which questions.

Review Collages

Midbrain

After teaching a new topic or subject, provide your students with magazines to look through and cut out both words and images that in some way represent the information that was taught. Then either verbally, or in written response, have the students explain the things they chose and how they represent the topic. You can do this in groups to add a limbic level to it.

ABCD Wall Jump

Midbrain

Designate each wall as being A, B, C, or D. Then ask multiple-choice questions. After asking the question, the students should jump and turn in the air to face the wall corresponding with the correct answer. These little jumps can be a great way to wake up the students and give you a quick idea of who understands the material.

Funny Hand Motion Responses

Midbrain

Work with your students to choose four different funny hand motions that would each symbolize an answer of A, B, C, or D. Then ask multiple-choice questions and have them respond with the corresponding hand motions. A key to making this work would be to have a little cheat sheet on the board to remind them which hand motion equals which letter. Secondly, if you can provide the questions and four possible answers on a PowerPoint displayed on the wall, they will be more likely to successfully manage the activity.

Snowball Fights

Adapted from *Energizing Brain Breaks*

Midbrain / Limbic

Give each student one or several sheets of paper. On each paper they should come up with their own review question / test question / essay question, etc. for the content you have been covering in class. Then split the class into two groups and let them crinkle up the papers into snowballs and have a 30 second snowball fight with the other half of the class. Once the time is up, have them each pick up however many snowballs they made and respond to whatever questions they happen to select. The snowball fight is fun and a great way to get blood pumping and exercise the midbrain, which should then prepare them to successfully answer the questions.

NeuroLogic® ACTIVITIES

Arm Responses

Midbrain / Limbic

Split your students in small groups of three or four. Ask them multiple-choice questions. As quickly as possible, the group needs to decide on the answer then work together to use their arms and make a giant version of that letter in the air. This is a great limbic exercise for getting students to work together in a safe way for healthy interaction.

Body-Tap Multiple Choice

Midbrain

Assign different body parts to different answers for multiple choice questions. For instance, head = A, knee = B, etc. When you ask the multiple-choice questions, the students have to tap the body part that corresponds with the correct answer. This is great to get a little bit of movement and will inevitably have the students crossing their midlines.

True False Balance

Midbrain

Ask true / false questions to review information you recently taught. If they balance on their left foot, it means the answer is true; if they balance on their right foot, it means the answer is false. This is a great way to quickly see how well your students are doing with the information and balancing is a great way to get their brains ready for learning.

Hop On The Right Answer

Midbrain

Spread students out across the room. Give each of them four pieces of paper, one of each multiple choice answer A, B, C, and D. As you ask questions, they need to jump on the correct answer. If you have a smaller class and want to make this a larger group activity, you could write the four possible answers on poster board or banner size pieces of paper and have the students hop over and onto the correct answer.

Five Step Conversations

Midbrain / Limbic

After teaching a new important concept, have each student stand up, take five large steps and partner up with whomever they are standing closest to. In their pairs, have one of them re-explain this new concept. The other person then either clarifies if they see it differently or agrees with how it was explained. This is a great way to get the students out of their seats for a moment and to find out how much they really understand what you just taught.

Sitting Answers

Midbrain / Limbic

For review with multiple choice questions, make different sitting positions link to different multiple-choice answers. A = sitting on desk, B = sitting in chair, C = sitting in chair backward, D = sitting on floor. This is a fun review activity to get blood flowing and to use some large muscle movement.

Thumb-Ball For Learning

Midbrain

If you have never seen one before, thumb-balls are essentially stuffed mini soccer balls. You can purchase blank ones or get them with questions written on them. I recommend purchasing blank ones or a similar style ball that is blank, and fill in each hexagon with a number. Then for each number on the ball, write one review question. Throw the ball around the room. Whatever number your left thumb is on when you catch the ball is the question you need to answer. You will inevitably get some repeats, but that repetition is great for students to learn effectively.

Move An Object To The Answer

Midbrain / Limbic

Have multiple-choice questions where each corner of the room represents one of the potential answers. Choose an object in the room, it could be a textbook, chair, stuffed animal, etc. The goal is to move the object so that it touches the corner that corresponds with the correct answer. The catch is that you cannot throw the object, it cannot touch the floor, and once you're touching it, you may not take any steps. The class needs to work together to not only figure out the correct answer, but creatively work together to get the object to where it should be. You can add a little tension by making this a timed event.

Large Dice Review

Midbrain

You can buy a large foam die or you can make a large die with a cardboard box. Create questions that correspond to numbers 1-6 and have students roll the die and answer the questions. Sometimes I make this a full class timed event where they have 4 minutes to get as many points as they can; they get the number on the die as points if they answer correctly. Add up the scores at the end. Play multiple times and encourage students to beat their last score.

Exercise Responses

Midbrain

If you have a class that does not mind a little bit of exercise, create a multiple choice review activity where each letter answer corresponds with an exercise. Example: A = push-up, B = jumping jack, etc. Instead of verbally answering the questions, allow the students to answer with physical movement. This will definitely help them wake up and get their brains ready for work.

Jenga Facts

Midbrain

Set up a traditional Jenga game and pick your students' turn orders. Before each turn, ask a review question. If they answer correctly, they can pull out a piece with their dominant hand. If they answer incorrectly, they need to use their non-dominant hand. Try other versions where they need to do it with their eyes shut, or they need to pick outside pieces if they get the questions wrong.

The Matching March

Midbrain

Supply students with index cards or small pieces of paper with words or images related to what you have been learning in class. It could be vocabulary words, formulas, math problems, periodic elements, etc. Then around the room, hang things that would match such as definitions, answers, etc. The students walk around the room and tape their cards to the corresponding match.

Banner Answers

Midbrain / Limbic

Give your students a few minutes with large pieces of paper to make separate banners for each of the major terms you are studying in class. In addition to writing the term really big on the banner, they can write some facts or notes about the term or doodles that represent the term. Once the banners are made, ask the class review questions. As a class, they need to pick and hold up the banner with the correct answer on it.

Putty Answers

Midbrain

Ask multiple-choice questions to review the information you have been covering in class. Instead of having the class responds out loud, give them each putty or playdough and let them mold the letter that corresponds with the correct answer. This is a great non-threatening way to learn if your students know the information you are covering. As long as you are walking around the room, you will quickly see who is immediately molding the correct answer, and who is looking around to see what others are molding before they begin to answer. You can also do this with pipe cleaners or other similar objects if you don't have putty.

Bottom Of The Foot Test Notes

Midbrain

It is not a rare practice for teachers to allow students to use an index card with notes on it to help while taking a test. If this is something you already do, consider having your students tape their notes to the bottom of their foot. Whenever they want to reference their notes, they need to stretch their foot up to read it. The goofiness of this may be enough to lighten some of the tension that comes with tests, and the stretching and bending to read their notes can be a great way to activate the midbrain. This is definitely one where it is important to know your students so you know if they will get frustrated or enjoy it, or if they can even physically bend their foot up in that way.

References

The following activities were adapted from *Brain Gym®* and are used with permission from the Educational Kinesiology Foundation, Santa Barbara, California. The descriptions of the exercises have been slightly modified. For more information about the Brain Gym program, visit www.braingym.org.

■ **Hook-Ups** ■ **Lazy 8's**

Dennison, P. E., Dennison, G. E., & Dennison, G. E. (2010). *Brain gym: teacher's edition.* Ventura, CA: Edu-Kinesthetics.

The following activities were adapted from *Doodles, Dances, and Ditties* and are used with permission from Mount Saint Vincent. For more information, visit: www.msvhome.org.

■ **Square Breathing** ■ **Six Second Count Breathing** ■ **Humming** ■ **Blowing Bubbles** ■ **Air Letter Stories** ■ **Mirroring** ■ **Lions Breath** ■ **Wake Up Breathing** ■ **Tap Your Tude** ■ **Imaginary Catch**

Hiebert, M., Platt, J., Schpok, K., & Whitesel, J. (2013). *Doodles, dances & ditties: a trauma-informed somatosenory handbook.* Denver, CO: Mount Saint Vincent Home.

The following activities were adapted from *Energizing Brain Breaks* and are used with permission from David Sladkey. For more information about Energizing Brain Breaks visit www.energizingbrainbreaks.com

■ **Opposite Thumb Twiddles** ■ **Hand Crossing Mix-up** ■ **Paper Balance** ■ **Thumb Pinkie Switch** ■ **Nose and Ear Reversal** ■ **ABC/123** ■ **Twisted Hands** ■ **Opposite Arm Rolls** ■ **Gotchya** ■ **Make it Snow** ■ **Snowball Questions** ■ **Snowball Fights**

Sladkey, D. (2013). *Energizing brain breaks.* Thousand Oaks, CA: Corwin.

For more information on Bruce Perry and The Child Trauma Academy, visit: www.childtrauma.org

To purchase a thumball, visit: www.thumball.com